HER MAJESTY THE
QUEEN
AS SEEN BY mac

Stan McMurtry mac
Edited by Mark Bryant

ROBINSON

For Nutmeg. The bravest and loveliest girl in my world.

ROBINSON

First published in Great Britain in 2016 by Robinson

3 5 7 9 10 8 6 4 2

Cartoons and Introduction copyright © Stan McMurtry, 2016

Selection and texts copyright © Mark Bryant, 2016

The moral rights of the authors have been asserted.

The drawing on p. i reproduced from *25 Years of MAC*.

A CIP catalogue record for this book is available from the British Library.

ISBN: 978-1-47213-964-1

Typeset by Design 23

Printed and bound in Great Britain by Bell & Bain Ltd

Papers used by Robinson are from well-managed forests and other responsible sources.

Robinson
An imprint of
Little, Brown Book Group
Carmelite House
50 Victoria Embankment
London EC4Y 0DZ

An Hachette UK Company

www.hachette.co.uk

www.littlebrown.co.uk

INTRODUCTION

Not many people are lucky enough to meet the Queen, so I count myself as very, very lucky.

Five years ago, Labour Prime Minister Tony Blair unexpectedly (because I hadn't been kind to him in several of my cartoons) decided to put my name forward for an MBE for services to the newspaper industry.

So I travelled, rather nervously, with my wife, Liz, and grown-up children, Karen and Andy, to Buckingham Palace and joined a very long line of people eagerly queuing up to meet Her Majesty and be presented with their gongs.

When it was my turn I was rewarded not only with my MBE medal but also a beautiful smile and a warm handshake. She is a remarkable woman, standing as she did for two or three hours and greeting everyone with the same friendliness that I received.

During the few words that we exchanged, she revealed that she and her husband, Prince Philip, enjoy looking at newspaper cartoons and that she particularly liked it when I drew the royal corgis. Since that day the corgis have always appeared in my cartoons featuring her.

Here is a selection of my royal cartoons going back throughout my time at the *Daily Mail*. I hope you'll enjoy them.

Following the attempted kidnapping of Princess Anne in The Mall in March 1974, extra security was introduced for the Royal Family. Meanwhile, Labour Chancellor Denis Healey introduced a new wealth tax to 'Soak the Rich'.

'Do you think this really IS extra security? Or is it Denis Healey making sure we don't escape before Tuesday?' *25 March 1974*

At a State Opening of Parliament during Harold Wilson's premiership, the media were full of stories about the Labour PM's business affairs. Was this a smear campaign? Mysteriously his income-tax papers disappeared . . .

'. . . and my total earnings for 1973–4 were . . . oh dear, I seem to have someone's tax forms mixed up with my speech.' *27 October 1974*

In a notorious lapse of royal security, a 33-year-old man broke into Buckingham Palace and entered the Queen's bedroom before being arrested. It later emerged that the intruder had tripped an alarm but the police had turned it off, thinking it was faulty.

'Dorothy, it's the lady down the road. She's going out for a while – can we keep an eye on the house?' *14 July 1982*

The pound fell to its lowest rate ever against the dollar in February 1985.

'Do something! – You're supposed to know all about gravity!' *14 January 1985*

On the third day of her official tour of New Zealand, the Queen was hit by an egg thrown by a female demonstrator in Auckland who was protesting against a treaty signed by the British and New Zealand's native Maoris 146 years earlier.

'Thank you, Perkins, that will be all – I think we're ready for them tomorrow.' *25 February 1986*

Royal couturier Sir Hardy Amies revealed that Her Majesty has a keen eye for a bargain.

'Oh dear, I hope she's not going to keep moaning about the prices again.' *22 May 1990*

A survey of the world's richest women showed that the Queen still led the field with assets of £6.6 billion and an estimated daily income of £1.8 million, reopening the media debate regarding her exemption from taxation.

'Philip, have you been at my purse? – I'm £1.27 short!' *5 February 1991*

The *Sunday Times* attacked the younger royals for 'parading a mixture of upper-class decadence and insensitivity' with regard to the Gulf War.

'Thank you, ma'am, but honestly, we feel the Royal Family is doing quite enough for the war effort . . .'
12 February 1991

A paternity suit filed in New Zealand against Captain Mark Phillips, estranged husband of the Princess Royal, caused problems at Buckingham Palace.

'Frankly, Mother, we feel you're worrying too much about any fresh scandals hitting the family.' *26 March 1991*

The 24-year-old daughter of a Buckingham Palace clerk, living in the Royal Mews,
was arrested following a police investigation into a drugs ring.

'Well, they don't normally behave like this after a Bob Martin's conditioning powder . . . ' *22 October 1991*

The Queen's Speech at the State Opening of Parliament set out the new government's agenda, including a National Lottery by 1994 which would raise more than £1 billion a year to fund the arts, sports, charities and tourism.

' . . . And now, in accordance with my government's wishes – eyes down for a full house . . .
clickety click, sixty-six . . . ' *7 May 1992*

The Queen agreed to pay income and capital gains tax for the first time, becoming the
first British monarch to do so since 1931.

'It's worth a try, I suppose, but I don't think the income tax man will be fooled.' *28 August 1992*

After a troubled year for the Royal Family, capped by a devastating fire at Windsor Castle, the Queen's speech at a banquet celebrating the 40th anniversary of her accession described 1992 as an 'annus horribilis'.

'Oh, come on, Arthur. She's had an absolutely horrid year.' *26 November 1992*

For the first time in history, Buckingham Palace opened its doors to the public in an effort
to raise money for the restoration of Windsor Castle.

'Oh, stop grumbling. We went round their house on Saturday.' *9 August 1993*

A 30-year-old American stuntman piloted a motorised parachute on to the roof of Buckingham Palace.
He was naked and covered in bright green paint when arrested by armed police.

'Hello, Security?' *7 February 1994*

As the Queen prepared for Britain's first royal visit to Russia in seventy-seven years, forensic tests on human remains proved conclusively that Tsar Nicholas II, George V's second cousin, had been murdered.

'Why not let bygones be bygones when you go, dear? President Yeltsin had nothing to do with your grandfather's second cousin . . .' *18 February 1994*

The Duchess of York turned down an offer to play the part of Boadicea, the tempestuous red-haired Queen of the Iceni, in a new £14 million film to be directed by Ken Russell.

'Mr Russell loved the wig, says thanks for the offer and he'll let you know, Your Majesty.' *23 May 1994*

In a TV documentary to mark the 25th anniversary of his investiture, the Prince of Wales said that as king of a multicultural Britain he would wish to be seen as defender of all faiths, not just the Church of England.

'Good morning, Charles – and which faith are we defending today?' *27 June 1994*

Buckingham Palace servants threatened to walk out midway through an official state dinner in protest against a new royal household pay-plan announced by Major Sir Shane Blewitt, Keeper of the Privy Purse.

'Still having trouble with your staff about pay then, ma'am?' *5 August 1994*

Disgraced fugitive banker Nick Leeson was arrested at Frankfurt Airport en route to London.
It was also revealed that some of Her Majesty's financial affairs had been managed by his company, Baring Brothers.

'Please don't be too hard on the lad – I want him to be my house guest.' *3 March 1995*

Faced with demands to cut costs, Buckingham Palace announced plans to rent out former royal staff and pensioners' quarters at Hampton Court.

'You didn't tell me you were doing bed and breakfast here at the Palace as well . . . ' *13 April 1995*

Actress Joanna Lumley, who played the flamboyant champagne-drinking character Patsy in BBC TV's award-winning comedy series *Absolutely Fabulous*, received an OBE at Buckingham Palace.

'I expect it was Absolutely Fabulous meeting Joanna Lumley, wasn't it, darling? Darling?' *4 May 1995*

A hospital employee from Norfolk tried unsuccessfully to sell the *Sun* a 17-minute recording of a phone conversation between Prince Philip and his friend, Lady Romsey, prompting speculation about the nature of their relationship.

'**Yes, privacy at last. They finally caught whoever it was that was taping our phone calls . . .** ' *1 February 1996*

In the first John Smith Memorial Lecture, Labour Party leader Tony Blair set out his plans for a future Labour government, which would include radical reforms to the House of Lords.

'Remember the good old days of 1996 . . . just before Tony Blair scrapped all hereditary titles?' *9 February 1996*

Various members of the Royal Family have asked MAC for the originals of his cartoons over the years, but he was especially pleased to have a request for this one from Her Majesty when security was tightened dramatically in 1996.

'I feel sorry for the corgis.' *27 February 1996*

As the trials and tribulations continued amongst the junior members
of the Royal Family, the Queen celebrated her 70th birthday.

'All our children and their spouses to Jupiter? Oh, Philip. You spoil me . . . ' *22 April 1996*

Antony Williams's controversial new portrait of the Queen went on show at the Mall Galleries in London. The unflattering picture showed the Queen with a careworn, unsmiling face and thick fingers.

'Well done, Charles. I should've got you to paint it in the first place.' *10 May 1996*

In what many saw as a deliberate rebuff for failing to inform the Palace about a damaging *Panorama* interview with Princess Diana, it was announced that the BBC would no longer have a monopoly to broadcast the Queen's Christmas message.

'There are only 152 shopping days till my Christmas speech. Why not treat oneself to the fresh, zingy taste of real coffee and one's corgis to munchy-crunchy Doggy Mix . . . ?' *26 July 1996*

As Labour prepared to write their first Queen's Speech for eighteen years, a special photo-call of the party's 101 female MPs – dubbed 'Blair's Babes' – was held on the steps of Church House, Westminster.

'I approve of most of it, Mr Blair. But I think we'll continue to call it The Queen's Speech.' *8 May 1997*

When Gordon Brown made his first speech as Chancellor at the Mansion House
he broke with tradition by not wearing white tie and tails.

' . . . then just as we were leaving, what a relief – Tony whispered in my ear, "There's no need to dress
quite so formally in future".' *15 May 1997*

During the Queen's tour of India to mark the 50th anniversary of Independence, a speech she had prepared to give at a banquet in Chennai, formerly Madras, was cancelled.

'Won't keep you long. She's determined not to waste that speech which was cancelled in Madras.' *20 October 1997*

The Government announced that the Grade One-listed Admiralty Arch building near Buckingham Palace
was to be turned into a cold-weather shelter for up to sixty young homeless people.

'I say, you up there. Will you turn that music down? One is trying to get some sleep.'
30 October 1997

As part of the Golden Wedding anniversary celebrations for the Queen and Prince Philip, a 'People's Banquet' was held for 350 guests during which commoners sat with royalty.

'Great time, Liz and Phil. Don't forget. For next year's people's banquet it's everyone round to our place.'
21 November 1997

A man attending an investiture at Buckingham Palace needed nine stitches after being struck by ceiling plaster. It was also revealed for the first time that Camilla Parker Bowles had regularly stayed overnight at nearby St James's Palace.

'Nip upstairs and tell Charles and Camilla to stop whatever they're doing immediately.' *5 March 1998*

War veterans, including Prince Philip – President of the Burma Star Association – were unhappy about the Queen's decision to confer the Order of the Garter on Japanese Emperor Akihito during his official visit to the UK.

'Thanks for the advice, Philip. But I'll just be giving the emperor the usual light tap on the shoulder.' *14 May 1998*

In a remarkable break with decorum, the Queen, a 72-year-old grandmother, sprinted across the paddock to watch Prince Philip performing in the Asprey's Carriage Driving Grand Prix at the Royal Windsor Horse Show.

'Let's hope this new running thing is only going to be a passing phase.' *19 May 1998*

During a visit to Glasgow, Her Majesty had tea at the housing association home of Mrs Susan McCarron on the city's Craigdale estate, demonstrating the new openness and accessibility of the monarchy.

'I promise you, this is the last reassurance to the public that we're "in touch", then we'll go home.' *9 July 1999*

The Countess of Wessex upset the Royal Family and anti-fur campaigners alike when she accepted lavish hospitality during a business weekend in St Moritz, Switzerland, and was photographed wearing a red fox-fur hat.

'Do you hear me, Sophie? Get back from St Moritz immediately and bring those furs with you.' *3 February 2000*

The Queen officially opened the Tate Modern gallery of modern art in the former Bankside power station on the south bank of the Thames.

'. . . and then I was shown a Damien Hirst animal sawn in half. Well, honestly. Even I could do that.' *12 May 2000*

Broadcasters hit the headlines when BBC chiefs refused to screen live coverage of the pageant to celebrate the 100th birthday of the Queen Mother because it clashed with *Neighbours*. Channel 5 was also criticised for showing too much soft porn.

'Wonderful news, everybody. I've just given exclusive rights to Channel Five – But we've all got to take our clothes off.' *15 May 2000*

The Queen finally gave official recognition to Camilla Parker Bowles as the consort of Prince Charles when she met and spoke to her at a party for ex-King Constantine of Greece which the Prince of Wales hosted at Highgrove House in Gloucestershire.

'It's Mrs Parker Bowles, ma'am. Now that you've broken the ice, how do you fancy a girly night out down at her local?' *5 June 2000*

The row about the Royal Family and bloodsports was reignited when the Queen was photographed wringing the neck of a pheasant injured during a shoot at Sandringham.

'Don't worry. You've got five seconds' start and if it's not a clean shot my wife wrings your neck.' *20 November 2000*

Judith Keppel became the first contestant to win £1 million on the TV quiz show *Who Wants to Be a Millionaire*. A relation of Alice Keppel, mistress of Edward VII, she is also a cousin of Camilla Parker Bowles.

'. . . And on tonight's programme we have Charles from Gloucestershire, Elizabeth from Windsor, Philip from Greece, Anne from . . .' *21 November 2000*

Eighteen-year-old Prince William went on a three-and-a-half month tour of southern Africa during his 'gap year' between leaving Eton and starting his degree course at St Andrew's University in Scotland.

'Such a thoughtful boy. He couldn't bear to know we were short of meat.' *5 March 2001*

As many livestock farmers faced ruin from the foot-and-mouth epidemic, Prince Charles personally pledged £500,000 from sales of his Duchy Original products and the Duke of Cornwall's Benevolent Fund to charities directly connected with farmers.

'Nice to see the royals are doing all they can for the farmers.' *16 March 2001*

Prince Edward and Sophie – who had referred to the Queen as 'the old dear' – were summoned to Buckingham Palace after it was claimed that they were using tax-payer-funded state visits to drum up business for Edward's ailing TV company, Ardent.

'Edward. Can you and Sophie pop round again? The old dear would like another word.' *6 April 2001*

The Countess of Wessex later fell victim to a *News of the World* 'fake sheikh' sting, which showed that she had used her royal contacts to promote her PR company. Meanwhile, *The Weakest Link* quiz appeared on US TV for the first time.

'So, Sophie. After that absolutely abysmal performance, you are the weakest link – goodbye.' *9 April 2001*

The *Spectator*, quoting a 'well-informed Palace observer', claimed that the Queen had agreed to the marriage of Prince Charles and Camilla Parker Bowles after the Golden Jubilee celebrations in 2002, but added that she could not herself become queen.

'Hoskins. Retrieve one's hat from Mrs Parker Bowles and escort her from the premises, will you?' *17 August 2001*

Princess Diana's former butler, Paul Burrell, appeared in court charged with stealing more than four hundred personal items from her worth an estimated £6 million.

'My suspicions about Wilkinson deepen – he's just handed me a ransom note for the corgis.' *20 August 2001*

As anthrax cases in the US began to rise, the British Government revealed that it only had enough stock of the antidote drug doxycycline to treat two million people. (This cartoon is also owned by the Queen.)

'Don't drink that one, Mother. It's our anti-anthrax vaccine.' *16 October 2001*

In a day of visits to celebrate the achievements of the broadcasting industry, the Queen and Prince Philip visited ITN, CNN, the BBC World Service and the set of the TV soap *EastEnders* at Elstree Studios in Hertfordshire.

**'Stone me, Benskin. We've been goin' round the bleedin' TV studios all day and we're knackered.
Pour us a couple of pints and 'ave one yourself.'** *29 November 2001*

In the latest in a series of disclosures by junior members of the Royal Family, a new biography of Her Majesty by journalist Graham Turner alleged that there had been deep rifts between the Prince of Wales and his parents.

'You heard your father! All you have to do is tell the newspapers what wonderful parents you have and you're free.'
10 January 2002

A 27-year-old male streaker from North Shields, with 'Rude Britannia' tattooed on his buttocks, ran beside the Queen's car for fifty yards as she drove to St Mary's Cathedral, Newcastle upon Tyne, to unveil a statue in honour of the late Cardinal Basil Hume.

'There was a streaker? Goodness me, I must be getting old. I didn't notice.' *9 May 2002*

The celebrations to mark the Queen's Golden Jubilee included classical and pop music concerts at Buckingham Palace. Among those performing were Cliff Richard, Elton John and Tom Jones.

'Do stop fidgeting, Philip. I'm told it will be expected of one to throw undergarments at Tom Jones when he sings tonight.' *3 June 2002*

Following the pop concert, attended by twelve thousand people with a million more outside watching on giant screens, the final day of the Jubilee celebrations included a ceremonial procession from Buckingham Palace to St Paul's Cathedral.

'Only nine hours, thirty-five minutes and eleven seconds to go . . .' *4 June 2002*

The all-party House of Commons Public Accounts Committee proposed scrapping the Royal Train – which cost taxpayers more than £700,000 a year and was only used for fifteen journeys in 2001 – thereby ending 160 years of privileged rail travel for the monarchy.

'*Now* what has New Labour done? First they scrap *Britannia*, then the Royal Train . . .' *8 July 2002*

The nation was rocked by rumours of a gay sex ring amongst servants at Buckingham Palace.

'The Queen? – Which one do you want?' *8 November 2002*

Buckingham Palace announced that it had appointed Sir Michael Peat, the Prince of Wales's chief courtier, to head an investigation into claims that a number of royal servants had plundered memorabilia worth millions of pounds from the Royal Family.

'A Chippendale table, ma'am? Are you sure? I don't remember a table being there.' *18 November 2002*

The *Sunday Times*'s annual 'Rich List' revealed that 37-year-old J.K.Rowling, author of the Harry Potter children's books, was Britain's wealthiest self-made woman, with a personal fortune of £280 million, making her richer than the Queen.

'. . . "Aha," cried Harry Windsor, stubbing out his fag and climbing on to his chauffeur-driven broomstick . . . '
28 April 2003

Two of the daughters of President Saddam Hussein of Iraq sought asylum in the UK, claiming that as their husbands – both former Saddam aides – had been executed for passing secrets to the West, they would face persecution and even death if they remained in Iraq.

'Look. One is terribly sorry that Blair bombed your palaces, but you're not having this one – now clear orf.' *3 June 2003*

As further extracts were published from the memoirs of Princess Diana's butler, its author also claimed to know 'everything there is to know' about the Queen, whom he had served as a personal footman for ten years.

'That's Paul Burrell's house and we didn't see a thing, did we, Hawkins?' *29 October 2003*

After surgery to remove cartilage on her right knee in January, Her Majesty had a similar operation on her left knee. Meanwhile, England beat Australia 20-17 to win the Rugby World Cup final for the first time with a last-minute drop goal by Jonny Wilkinson.

'Never mind how soon I can resume my royal duties. When will I be able to practise drop-kicks again?'
11 December 2003

Children at a school on the Royal Sandringham estate in Norfolk were reduced to tears when a shooting party – believed to have included Prince Philip – sent dead pheasants raining down in a field just yards from their playground.

'Do stop moaning, Philip. This way you won't be upsetting the local schoolchildren. All right, Chivers, release the budgie.' *15 January 2004*

Less than a year after a 'comedy terrorist' gatecrashed Prince William's 21st birthday party, there was another royal intruder scare at Windsor Castle when a man posing as a plain-clothes' detective allegedly came within yards of the Queen's bedroom.

'Have a word with security, Philip. On Monday somebody got within yards of me, pretending to be a policeman.' *19 May 2004*

At a ceremony in Balaklava, Ukraine, to mark the 150th anniversary of the Charge of the Light Brigade, the 83-year-old Duke of Edinburgh wore sunglasses to cover up a black eye he claimed was the result of a fall in the bathroom of his hotel.

'I'll tell everyone he slipped in the bath. But I'm warning you, Harry – don't you dare take your grandfather nightclubbing again!' *27 October 2004*

In an unfair dismissal case brought by a former member of Prince Charles's household, it was revealed that the Prince had said: 'What is it that makes everyone seem to think they are qualified to do things beyond their technical capabilities?'

'You want to be King? What is it, Charles, that makes everyone think they are qualified to do things far beyond their capabilities?' *19 November 2004*

The Government announced plans to introduce compulsory identity cards to help guard against terrorism. Meanwhile, Buckingham Palace's security was tightened after another fathers' rights protester scaled a twenty-foot gatepost and chained himself to it.

'Come on, come on. How are we to know you're not al-Qaeda? – Where's your ID card?' *24 November 2004*

After much discussion, it was agreed that, following their marriage, Prince Charles's wife would be addressed as HRH the Duchess of Cornwall, but it was still unclear whether she would become Queen if and when Prince Charles accedes to the throne.

'It's your mother, sir. Did Mrs Parker Bowles accidentally pick up the wrong hat when you last visited?'
15 February 2005

Buckingham Palace reported that Her Majesty would not attend Prince Charles's civil wedding to Camilla Parker Bowles at the Guildhall, Windsor, but added that she would be present at a blessing service in Windsor Castle after the ceremony.

'Picture their faces, ma'am, if at the last moment you burst out of the cake shouting, "Surprise, surprise!"'
24 February 2005

After considerable debate, Constitutional Affairs Minister Christopher Leslie confirmed that Camilla
Parker Bowles would become Queen if and when Prince Charles accedes to the throne.

'Are you absolutely sure she'd get custody of the corgis?' *23 March 2005*

Following a risk-assessment study on Prince Charles's new wife, the Duchess of Cornwall was given a new SAS-trained female police bodyguard.

'Charles, dear. Would you tell Camilla that her in-laws have popped in for a cup of tea and to mention this to her new bodyguard?' *27 April 2005*

Royal Ascot was moved to York to allow the racecourse to be redeveloped.

'Oh. You don't understand one's accent? – Try this: By 'eck, lad. T'bugger coom in fust.
Fifty smackers or ah'll set t'corgi on tha!' *16 June 2005*

The annual Royal Public Finances Report revealed that Prince Charles and Prince Andrew spent £1.5 million of taxpayers' money on travel in 2014, while the Queen and Prince Philip only spent £392,000.

'Another drain on the public purse! Do you know how much those tandems cost?' *23 June 2005*

The Queen celebrated her 80th birthday. She received more than 20,000 birthday cards.

'If that's the post, Philip, dear, will you see if there are any cards for me?' *21 April 2006*

Norwich Crown Court heard the case of a 38-year-old conman from Cambridgeshire who had faked letters of recommendation to receive an MBE from Her Majesty in 2003.

'We've already checked for conmen, ma'am. I think you'll find that one was genuine.' *31 August 2006*

The Queen opened the new session of Parliament. Meanwhile, in what many saw as another intrusion of the 'nanny state', the Government introduced a National Academy for Parenting Practitioners to make sure parents read and sang nursery rhymes to their young children.

' . . . and for any children listening, my government have asked me to sing . . . Baa Baa Black Sheep Have You Any Wool . . . ' *15 November 2006*

Dame Helen Mirren won the award for Best Actress at Hollywood's Golden Globe Awards for her role in the film *The Queen* about the life of Elizabeth II.

'How terribly exciting, Philip, dear. They're making a film called *Helen Mirren* and I've been offered the part.' *17 January 2007*

The Queen later went on to win more many more awards, including Best Actress for Helen Mirren at the Oscars.

'Personally, I thought the dog who played me was rubbish.' *27 February 2007*

Shortly before he was due to be posted to Iraq, 22-year-old Prince Harry was reprimanded by superior officers in his regiment, the Blues & Royals, after a series of incidents in which he was found to be drunk and disorderly in public places.

'Oh, really? Well I brought my granny along, too, and we both think your conduct has been appalling!' *3 April 2007*

The 2007 Wimbledon tennis tournament got off to a tense start as Britain's Naomi Cavaday narrowly failed to win two match points against 1997 champion Martina Hingis. Meanwhile, Tony Blair finally resigned as Prime Minister and was succeeded by Gordon Brown.

'Gentlemen. Her Majesty doesn't want to be disturbed right now . . . but there is a message.' *27 June 2007*

Despite the fact that a large piece of falling masonry had recently narrowly missed hitting Princess Anne's car, Buckingham Palace was told that there would be no increase to the annual public grant of £15 million for maintaining Britain's crumbling royal palaces.

'Yes, Mr Brown. More falling masonry . . . my husband has just gone up to inspect the damage.' *29 June 2007*

As royal residences continued to deteriorate, the Government turned down the Queen's request for an additional £3 million for repairs.

'Damned cheek! No money for Palace repairs – only a note from Brown saying,
"You can do it if you B&Q it."' *8 February 2008*

The Government announced that it planned to build three million new homes by 2020. Meanwhile, a report by the Campaign to Protect Rural England claimed that 30,000 acres of Green Belt land around cities had been lost since Labour came to power.

'Mrs Higgins from the flats next door says can she borrow a cup of sugar till she's been down the shops?' *8 May 2008*

Buckingham Palace officials objected when unapproved photographs of senior members of the Royal Family appeared in *Hello!* magazine's coverage of the marriage of Princess Anne's son Peter Phillips in St George's Chapel, Windsor.

'The centrefold editor of *Playboy* magazine on the phone for you, ma'am.' *22 May 2008*

During a visit to the London School of Economics, the Queen, whose personal fortune was estimated to have fallen £25 million in the so-called 'credit crunch', wanted to know why no one saw the financial crisis coming.

'It's getting a bit cold in here – time to change the corgis.' *26 September 2008*

Buckingham Palace officials were displeased to learn that the French Government had not invited the Queen to the 65th anniversary of D-Day events in Normandy. However, President Sarkozy (whose wife, Carla, is a former model) had invited US President Barack Obama.

'Damned cheek! I know what I'd like to do to the Sarkozys. What about you, Philip?' *28 May 2009*

A group of eminent economists wrote to Her Majesty explaining why the timing, extent and severity of the recession had been unexpected. In April 2008, Her Majesty's private wealth was estimated to be £320 million by *Forbes* magazine.

'Oh, no! Not *Fricassée de poulet Cardinal La Balue* with asparagus tips and sautéed potatoes again!' *30 June 2009*

Prince Andrew was criticised for wasting taxpayers' money by flying short distances by helicopter in his role as the UK's special representative for trade and industry rather than using public transport. He had earlier used a helicopter to take him from Windsor to a golf course in Kent for a party.

'Yes. It's Andrew all right. Off to some golf course I expect . . . take aim, Philip.' *1 July 2009*

In a new drive to employ minorities, the Metropolitan Police posted an advertisement inviting gay, lesbian and transgender officers to apply to protect the Queen and Royal Family at Buckingham Palace, Windsor Castle and Balmoral.

'Before you turn on the charm, Philip, that's Nigel my new bodyguard.'
24 September 2009

Labour Prime Minister Gordon Brown introduced free social care for the elderly and most needy pensioners in their own homes, paid for by the Department of Health and local authorities.

'Call out the guard, Philip! There's a deranged person here who keeps saying, "Get yer kit off, it's bathtime".' *19 November 2009*

The Duchess of York, exposed in a televised 'sting' set up by the *News of the World*, offered to arrange a meeting between a fake businessman and Prince Andrew for £500,000. Meanwhile, the Queen's Speech opened the new session of Parliament.

'That's right, ma'am. I bought a ticket from "Fergie Enterprises". Meet the Queen – a hundred quid.' *25 May 2010*

For the first time in twenty years, Her Majesty asked for a rise in her Civil List allowance to plug the gap in the royal household's finances. The shortfall of £6 million a year was being met by an emergency reserve due to run out in 2012.

'What does one want? . . . A £6 million rise! . . . When does one want it? . . . Before one's country goes broke!'
1 June 2010

The Queen was not spared in the Government's expenditure cuts and was informed that the royal budget would fall by 14 per cent over the next three years. Meanwhile, Manchester United striker Wayne Rooney agreed a new pay deal with the club for more than £10 million a year.

'We're saved! I've asked Wayne Rooney for a loan.' *22 October 2010*

Barely six weeks after the news of Prince William's engagement to Kate Middleton, his cousin Zara Phillips (daughter of the Princess Royal and Captain Mark Phillips) announced her plans to wed England rugby player, Mike Tindall.

'Two's enough for one year. I hope no one else is going to spring any surprises.' *23 December 2010*

Prince Andrew came under increasing pressure to resign as Britain's trade ambassador after it was discovered that he had links with a disgraced billionaire involved in a sex scandal who had also helped pay off some of the Duchess of York's debts.

'Be honest with me, Philip. Are you going after grouse, pheasant or Andrew?' *8 March 2011*

The Duke of Edinburgh celebrated his 90th birthday.

'And just think, Philip, dear. Only another ten years and you'll be getting a telegram from me.' *10 June 2011*

Shortly after the *News of the World* closed in the wake of a phone-hacking scandal, it was revealed that the paper had paid a corrupt Royal Protection Officer for highly sensitive details about the Queen, her close family and staff.

'That reminds me. Charles called but the new line was a bit faint so I've no idea what he wanted.' *13 July 2011*

Disgraced banker Sir Fred Goodwin, former head of the Royal Bank of Scotland – which had to be bailed out with taxpayers' money – faced calls to be stripped of his knighthood.

'I hope I'm here on the day – I've never seen a knighthood revoked before.' *20 January 2012*

In a statement to mark the start of her Diamond Jubilee year, the Queen – only the second monarch (after Queen Victoria) ever to celebrate sixty years on the British throne – vowed to serve her people for the rest of her life.

'Right. I've decided. After the Jubilee and the Olympics we slow down a bit.
What d'you think, Philip?' *7 February 2012*

At the State Opening of Parliament, the Queen's Speech outlining the Government's proposed reforms for the coming year lasted only fifteen minutes.

'It's the Prime Minister. To cut costs next year he wants me just to do it all on Facebook.' *10 May 2012*

The Queen celebrated her Diamond Jubilee with four days of televised events beginning with the River Thames Jubilee Pageant featuring one thousand boats from around the Commonwealth, the largest flotilla seen on the river in 350 years.

'OK, team. I've done my bit. Now who's going to volunteer for the Ceremonial Day and the RAF flypast?' *5 June 2012*

As Prince Philip was taken ill after the river pageant, the Queen was unaccompanied at other Jubilee events, including a concert outside Buckingham Palace, an RAF flypast, a fireworks display, the lighting of a beacon, a service at St Paul's Cathedral and a number of state receptions.

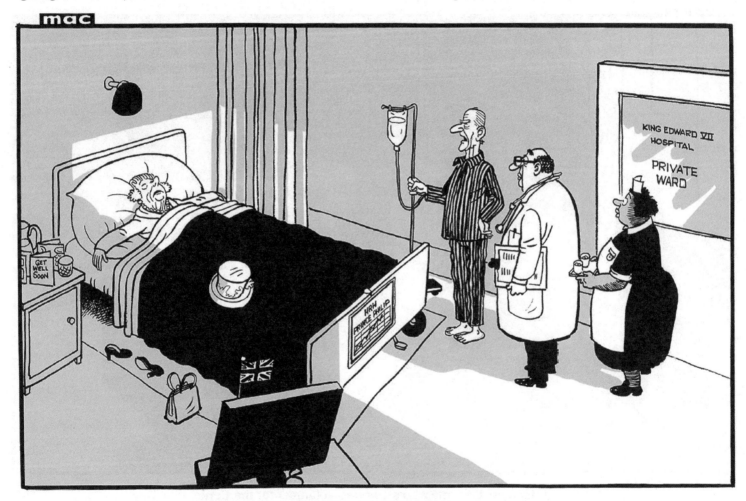

'First visit and all she said was "Move over".' *6 June 2012*

At the opening ceremony for the London Olympics, Her Majesty was shown leaving Buckingham Place in a helicopter with James Bond (played by Daniel Craig) and apparently parachuting out over the Olympic Park before entering the stadium to officially open the games.

'I expect there'll be quite a rush to get the empty seats.' *31 July 2012*

During a special reception at Buckingham Palace held by the Queen to honour Britain's Olympic and Paralympic stars, one of the athletes used her mobile phone to take a picture of one of the visitors' toilets and tweeted it to her followers.

'Lock the door after you. Some b***'s taken photographs of the visitors' loo!'** *26 October 2012*

Buckingham Palace announced that the Duke and Duchess of Cambridge were expecting their first child.

'Remind me again, dear. Is it knit one, purl one or knit two, purl four?' *5 December 2012*

To mark the 150th anniversary of the London Underground, Prince Charles and the Duchess of Cornwall travelled from Farringdon to King's Cross (one stop) on the Metropolitan Line.

'I don't understand. Charles and Camilla said it was quite jolly.' *1 February 2013*

The Queen, aged eighty-six, was admitted into hospital with a stomach bug.

'Listen . . . the national anthem . . . she must be leaving! – EVERYBODY UP!' *5 March 2013*

In Cairo, the Egyptian Army deposed the recently elected President Mohamed Morsi. Meanwhile, Prince Charles visited the set of the BBC's *Doctor Who* TV series in Cardiff to mark the 50th anniversary of the programme.

'Oh dear. A *coup d'état* in Egypt. Whatever next?' *5 July 2013*

There was an international media frenzy when the Duchess of Cambridge gave
birth to an 8lb 6oz baby boy, Prince George, at St Mary's Hospital in London.

**'It's so exciting. There's going to be photographic sessions, foreign dignitaries for the baby
to meet, concerts, Morris dancers . . . '** *23 July 2013*

Amongst a number of documents released by the Government to the National Archives under the '30-year rule' was a speech which the Queen might have delivered if Britain had found itself on the verge of nuclear war.

'Philip, dear. That was a nuclear war speech I might have had to make way back in 1983.' *2 August 2013*

Two heavily armed police mistook the Duke of York for an intruder while he was walking in the grounds of Buckingham Palace. Meanwhile, new official figures showed a dramatic increase in the use of tasers by police in the UK.

'One is walking one's dogs in one's garden – any other questions?' *10 September 2013*

An ITV documentary revealed that a new report by the Independent Drug Monitoring Unit estimated that 500,000 people grow cannabis at home in the UK, roughly one person on every street.

'It's a fair cop, ma'am. And I'd like thirty-seven other bedrooms taken into consideration.' *16 October 2013*

When the former England football captain, David Beckham OBE – renowned for his many body tattoos – finally retired, many were disappointed that he did not receive a knighthood in the New Years Honours List for his work as an ambassador for the 2012 London Olympics.

'I'm disappointed David Beckham's not on the list – I was hoping to show him my new tattoo.' *31 December 2013*

Her Majesty returned from an eight-week break on her Sandringham estate in Norfolk to find parts of Windsor flooded by the swollen River Thames.

'Ah. Here comes Benskin now – he's been walking the corgis.' *11 February 2014*

A special issue of *Hello!* magazine featured baby Mia and her proud parents, Zara Phillips and former England rugby captain, Mike Tindall MBE.

'Do stop fussing and get on with it – we didn't have this opportunity sixty-five years ago.' *26 February 2014*

At the beginning of a two-day visit to Northern Ireland, Prince Charles and the Duchess of Cornwall met a group of traditional straw-masked Irish Mummers at Enniskillen Castle Museum in Co. Fermanagh.

'Before you hand out the biscuits, are we absolutely sure they are Charles and Camilla?' *3 April 2014*

An advertisement for a part-time cleaner based at the royal residence of Holyroodhouse in Edinburgh stipulated that, as well as normal domestic duties, the successful applicant would have to pick sticky gum off the floor and furniture.

'Your job is to remove this disgusting bubble-gum and if you see who's dropping it to give them a good whack with your mop.' *3 October 2014*

Former Tory minister David Mellor was accused of abusive behaviour to a taxi-driver after visiting Buckingham Palace with his partner Lady Cobham, chairman of VisitEngland, who had just been awarded a CBE for her services to tourism.

'I'm sorry her day was ruined . . . No, I can't do it all again . . . Please don't swear . . .
Yes, I know who you are . . . Oh, really? . . . And the same to you, Mr Mellor!'
27 November 2014

The Prince Charles letters, known as 'black spider notes' because of his spindly handwriting, were written when he had been waiting more than half a century to take over the throne.

'... regarding your recent letter complaining about my rule and suggesting nice little retirement homes in Bournemouth – GET LOST! Yours affectionately, Mother.' *15 May 2015*

A *Sun* front-page headline 'Queen Backs Brexit', referring to alleged private comments attacking the EU made by Her Majesty, was deemed 'significantly misleading' by the Independent Press Standards Organisation.

'I assure you, William is not backing the EU. All members of the royal household are completely unbiased.' *18 February 2016*

Thirty-five-year-old Tom Hiddleston, star of the BBC spy series *The Night Manager*, became the latest leading man to appear bare-chested on TV. Meanwhile, UKIP leader, Nigel Farage, continued to campaign for Brexit in media coverage of the Referendum debate.

'So many bare-chested hunks on TV nowadays – shame Nigel Farage never takes his shirt off.' *10 March 2016*

During a garden party at Buckingham Palace, the Queen was filmed discussing President Xi Jinping of China's first state visit to Britain in 2015 and was overheard to say that Chinese officials had been 'very rude' to the British ambassador.

'I assure you, ambassador. My wife meant no offence to you slitty-eyed people.' *12 May 2016*

The nation went to the polls to vote in the Referendum on whether to Leave or Remain in the European Union. In the event the Leave voters won by 52 per cent to 48 per cent.

'It's crunch day, Philip. The nation decides who's in charge – me or Mrs Merkel.' *23 June 2016*

Outgoing Prime Minister David Cameron was accused of rewarding his political friends and cronies in his controversial resignation honours list.

'To be honest, love, it was a bit of a surprise for me, too. All I did was clean his shoes.' *3 August 2016*